Would You Believe?

by

RENÉE ALYSON

Would You Believe?

Copyright ©2022 by Renée Alyson
ISBN #979-8-9854594-3-2

Dedication ~

This testament of gratitude is for the Creator of life—the Heavens and the earth, of whom I received my very breath. He knew me in my mother's womb, even before the foundations of the world. Without my God—I would not have survived the many trials endured. Without a Savior, I would not be here today to be a witness to His unwavering love. Saying yes to Him has been the best decision of my life. Undoubtedly, the highest road on which to travel.

This book is dedicated to my beloved parents who are no longer with me. It is my blessed assurance they are standing in awe of His presence in the throne room of glory. The heavens are more beautiful today as my mother and father displayed the essence of beauty, inside and out.

This true account is a celebration for my precious Eliza McLemore who was eighty-eight when she went home to be with The Lord. Eliza was my spiritual mentor just after my heart was circumcised by the Holy Spirit. Considered a Five-Star General for The Lord—Eliza always heard His voice and obeyed His commands.

Accolades ~

I spent several years getting to know Renée Alyson. Then while in the depths of brain cancer, her marriage disintegrated. An overcomer is an understatement! A must-read book of courage and hope.

- Ann Platz Groton
Author, Speaker, and Designer

Wonderfullllllllll!

- Desiree Lyon
Global Director American Porphyria Foundation

Beautiful story!

- Rabbi Gabriel Simkin, Messianic Rabbi
Mishkan David Messianic Congregation

Accolades ~

Have you ever known a person who seems so strong—so enviably strong, that you think, "I wish I knew her secret? Or maybe you think, Hmmm, she must have had an easy life, no wonder she is so joyful." Would you believe such a person has pulled back the curtain to reveal the source of her strength? Renée is inviting you to walk through some of the harshest challenges this world can throw at us, and with her honesty, as she shares these struggles, you just might weep with her. Each page exudes her warmth, kindness, and vulnerability, as if you, the reader, were her best friend. As you travel with her through the turbulent, emotional, and physical upheavals of her life, her passionate longing bursts forth to share her "secret." I believe the reader who will venture with Renée through these pages will be encouraged and when she asks, Would You Believe? you will say, Yes, I do.

- Miriam Finesilver
Author of *Naomi, the Rabbi's Wife* and *The Apple of His Eye*

Dear Reader ~

This story is written with prayer, that you will garner the knowledge and wisdom of your own destiny, which is in the hands of God—the Creator of us all.

I pray you will glean from my book that abiding in Yeshua is not a turn-off—not stuffy or dogmatic (I remember thinking that way)—but you will discover as I have, abiding in Him is the coolest way to live.

Please hear the urgency of my heart as I yearn for those who don't yet know Messiah to turn back to the call of God, the Author and Finisher of our faith.

~ *Table of Contents* ~

PART ONE

PART TWO

PART ONE

Chapter 1: Would You Believe?

Friday, December 7, 2005

Having just rounded the corner from Peachtree Road to Piedmont Road in Buckhead—uptown Atlanta, my head was thrown back. I was out cold.

Traffic was jammed. Christmas was near. And the excitement of the season joined with the rush to find the perfect gift for the loved one was on everyone's mind. I never questioned celebrating this holiday. The reason may have very well been shallow as every year I couldn't wait to buy more colorful ornaments. *Colorful ornaments?*

<p style="text-align:center">~~~</p>

My only intent was to get through the onset of cars to reach I-400—the way home. I had just glanced at my watch. It was of the worst time of the day, nearing four p.m.—the worst time of year. I had made the last trip for the week to our new residence in town. It was a long day of packing boxes from our current home in Riverview Estates to Buckhead. We were relocating southbound, closer to the city of Atlanta.

The real estate agent showed us several impressive homes in Buckhead, but none included a location to park the cars. The old residences as huge as they were only had street parking. We were currently living in a large home with a substantial garage. And two Brittany spaniels and a Cavalier King Charles spaniel. They enjoyed the acre of flat green grass in our backyard along with a swimming pool—and a wooded park down the street. All on the Chattahoochee River. It was an exceptional existence for any dog, much less any human being.

Our search for a new home had become tiresome. But there was one more place our agent wanted to show us. Looking rather small from the outside, I wasn't convinced it would be right for us. It reminded me of a miniature version of my grandparent's home in Charlotte with its arched front door. Yet once inside it seemed to expand in every direction. I even got confused as to which way to go. Originally built in 1947, it had just been refurbished leaving a lot of the distinctive vintage features. I fell in love with the large master and fireplace with all the little nooks and crannies that were indicative of the era. The door to the main bedroom suite closed, making it private, leaving an ample long hallway with a large walk-in closet on one side. The intimate room had a small chute on the floor with a door handle that would send dirty clothes to a basket in the basement. A nifty feature. Across the wide hallway was the master bathroom—steam shower and large jacuzzi tub included.

Never lacking anything, I had lived this kind of lifestyle as I was growing up. The chef's kitchen was perfect. It felt like home. Large square quartz countertop with eight swivel chairs all around for dinner parties. On the meal prep side, the counter was equipped with a button that made the exhaust fan raise to remove grease and smoke odors. Brand new appliances with a sub-zero refrigerator. Even a Butler's pantry. Plus, two sets of French doors—one set from the kitchen, the other from the master bedroom. The doors led out to a partially screened-in patio; the large side opened to the plush landscaping where one could gaze at the flutter of leaves. What a sight to behold; bringing in the outdoors. There is something extravagant about God's creation of living greens—trees and branches with bright leaves quivering with the slightest puff of wind. It was intoxicating. The patio was the place to relax. It was stunning and all together quaint!

~~~

It was a dreary cold day. In a split second my head was thrown back, capsized while making the turn from one major street to the next. The guy behind me laid on his horn. He observed that my car seemed to be driving itself, off course. He pulled up beside me. What he witnessed sent him reeling. My body was convulsing over the steering wheel. He quickly got around me and let my car collide into
~~~

the back of his vehicle. After several failed attempts to break my windows, he stayed the length of time for the ambulance to make it through the stop-and-go traffic—and to be sure I got freed from my car which now served as a trap.

I was seizing for over a half-hour. (My witness informed me later.) No one ever seizes for that length of time without having a brain deficit or dying. I woke up to paramedics all around me.

~

Would You Believe
is timeless

~

Chapter 2: Would You Believe?

Tasting Blood ~ 1984

"A doctor? You have a doctor?"

Eyes wide open, my husband tore down the hall and disappeared from my sight. It was hard to focus. Heavy-eyed, I got out of bed and twirled around, unaware of my surroundings. My body was weak, legs crumbled beneath me. I swallowed blood. Propelled forward, I bashed my nose against the bathroom door which left a nasty bruise. Turned in the opposite direction, whirled around, and collapsed on the bed—falling into a coma-like sleep.

Just thirty years old, I was the perfect picture of health—I thought.

After going through multiple tests and exams the doctor's consensus was to put me on anti-convulsant medications for the moment—for the moment ended up being the next nineteen years.

~

Would You Believe
answers the question as to
why we are here

~

Chapter 3: Would You Believe?

BearPause ~ 2000

Some twenty years later, we were living in a large home on the Chattahoochee River and loving our home—and our lives.

Morris's brother had purchased a motorcycle dealership in Tennessee. My husband and his two brothers rode motorcycles throughout their lives. It was his chance to purchase another go-fast bike at a family discount. He picked out the fastest and coolest-looking one—a crotch rocket. Taking off lickety-split on the weekends on his new hotrod, I knew he needed to blow off steam from the work week. He tried to take me riding once but with no seatback, I felt vulnerable—nearly falling backward into oncoming cars.

While not aware of where he was cruising, he found us the greatest cabin. We purchased it! It was a couple of hours north of where we lived in the suburbs. Once we entered the Appalachian Mountains, and over the ridge—through coiled roads, valleys, wilderness, and forests there appeared, Trillium Road—named after a mountain flower. Having to hold on to the handrail above, the winding roads guiding the way to our destination—a D-Log cabin in Suches, Georgia we named BearPause. The isolated cabin was in the woods off a two-lane highway that led further north to the minuscule town of Blue Ridge—with only two traffic lights.

Seven small homes consisted of our little retreats—all built by different construction companies. Our cabin was next to last. The Appalachian Mountain trails just a couple of hundred feet out our front door. The Toccoa River out our back door. We could hear from the screened-in back porch, the trickling of water as it gushed its way over the rocks.

One of my favorite things was watching the hummingbirds as they battled each other for the sugar water out our back door—diving motors zooming all around.

There were several hiking trails almost visible from the gravel road. Just up a steep cliff was a fork that led to the many hiking paths. Our lives consisted of weekend hikes with the two Brittany's and the Cavalier King Charles. It was heaven for the pups. They could run free until we could just barely see them, then return to our sides. I remember thinking the Brittany's looked so tiny. They were no bigger than the size of my pinkie.

One afternoon around 4:30 on Friday we were halfway up to our cabin, just about to climb the mountain, and onto the top of the ridge.

"Morris, I'm not feeling right."

He was peering over at me.

"Do you want to turn around?" he uttered.

Not answering him right away—a slight pause, "No, I think I can make it." *Of course, I questioned myself.*

We got off I-400 at the end of the long highway that stretched from downtown Atlanta to the north, an hour's drive—rural territory, in the country. As we headed towards the mountain ridge, he kept looking over at me.

"You sure?"

The headache made me sick to my stomach. Brows knit—my body slumped against the window. Morris was concerned. Unable to answer him, he had already made up his mind. He pulled off the road before cell service would be unavailable for us. It proved to be a challenge to find a side street, away from this curvy two-lane road. He had the opportunity to swerve quickly to the right and off the highway. It was near 5:00 pm. I called Dr. Kellman's office to let them know what was going on. (They would shut their phones off any minute.) After explaining everything to Patty, the doctor's PA, she put me on hold to echo it back to Dr. Kellman.

"Is the cabin near a hospital?"

"Yes, about forty minutes to the nearest town."

Patty replied, "If it gets any worse, please go to the hospital. You are either having a stroke or a brain tumor."

Not hearing brain tumor, only stroke—I thought I was way too young to have a stroke.

Patty continued, "I'm going to call the MRI lab and have you booked. Call us first thing Monday morning to find out the schedule for your appointment."

~~~

We loved hiking in the fall—there was the distinct sound of crackling leaves under our boots. The crunch of the dried brown leaves gave us time to clear our minds—an entrancing activity that left us untroubled.
~~~

Laying on the sofa in front of the stone fireplace, warmed by the fire was my activity for this weekend in Suches. Morris took the dogs hiking and had a delightful time in the brisk air. A few hours later, I heard the front screen door blast open. The dogs ran inside—tongues rapidly going back and forth, ready to quench their thirsts. Morris, right behind them. He headed out to the porch to read the paper—The three dogs with their broad smiles were a pleasing sight. We had a happy family.

Before dusk, Morris went upstairs to shower in the loft bath. He came down and asked me, "Are you feeling any better?"

Again, a pause, "No, I'm not. In fact, I'm worse." I sat up from the sofa where I had spent the day. Hungry, I opened the refrigerator to see what I wanted to quell the hunger pangs. As I passed Morris heading back to the sofa, he had his arms out for me. I fell against his willing chest, wanting this weekend to be over.

Wednesday morning at 8:30 was my appointment. Still, ongoing headaches from last Friday to Wednesday. *Could this be a migraine?* The technician handling the appointment came to the room at the halfway point to inject me with contrast. She asked in a sympathetic tone, how I was feeling. *I knew that soft-hearted look.*

"You see something, don't you?"

The technician told me not to worry. My doctor would let me know if anything irregular showed on the MRI.

I couldn't wait to get in my car, knowing I would break down. *Maybe the technician was wrong. It's probably nothing?*

~

Would You Believe
tells who put us here

~

Chapter 4: Would You Believe?

Spring Frenzy ~ 2001

Easter or Passover was approaching. Unusual, this Holy Day known as Passover, the feast of unleavened bread, would come to mean so much to me later. Meanwhile, my husband's office enjoyed their Good Friday lunch. They clocked out early at 1:00 pm. It was an exhilarating time of year, and I was invited to join them.

While driving on I-400 to the city to make my way to this lunch celebration, I started having symptoms on the right side of my body. A numb sensation on my forearm and foot. A bright vertical green beam appeared in my right peripheral vision. Traveling at speeds up to 70 mph, I became cautious, about the symptoms—about crashing—trying desperately to make it through the rush of cars flying past me. *Could I make it to my destination?* The sensation of terror quickly rose from my gut to my throat. I thought about where to park—the tow zone. A strip of road designated for delivery trucks only. NO PARKING ZONE. Frazzled, I made the dreaded call—knowing this was not the best time to distract him from a lighthearted lunch with his staff. I was hesitant, but my situation could be critical. I was unable to put the pieces together. *What if I were sick?*

~~~

Morris answered my call, "Hi, are you on your way up?"

He was just sitting down to a cold beer. I had many spring lunches there in past years. On this day, the weather was crisp and clear—a gentle breeze blowing—skies vibrant blue without a cloud in sight. It should've been a pleasure for me, yet…I could hear
~~~

the background noise. They were all sitting outside on the patio, laughing and drinking—not to mention the awful stench of cigarette smoke that always made me cough.

"I'm not feeling right. There are some issues I'd like to talk to you about. Please come down. I want you to go to the doctor with me," I answered with a false sense of alarm—never wanting to think it was me who was sick. Little did I know, what was in store within the next few hours…

It would take a blow to my head to bring me to my knees.

"Why? What's the problem? I want to be here." I could hear a long sigh… Can you tell me why?"

In the worst way, he did not want to interrupt his good time to do something boring. He finally agreed and came down but seemed unwilling to go with me. He looked at me from the passenger window. Peering in, he saw the troubled look on my face and jumped into the passengers' seat. We discussed my concerns while driving. Still, he did not take them seriously. *I was never one to complain, so how could either of us know the seriousness of my situation.*

The doctor entered the room with a woosh. The PA was right behind him. He pulled up a stool, getting way too close to my face. Doctor Kellman spoke firm and direct. The news was going to be hard to spell out. It would cause my undoing—and knock my husband out cold.

He looked me in the eyes and said slowly, "We found something in your films. A large mass. I know this is shocking, but the good news is it's operable."

Go...od news?!?

"Wha...wha...what di... y... sa...y? Can you re...peat tha...ha," as my letters and partial words were fused together like heaving breaths of tidal waves.

"You have a large mass on your brain."

"No... no-ho... not me...no...noh...no no no..." Those words were like poison to my soul.

"You must be mistaken! Not mee...hee... I cried out."

I fell apart. My hands went straight to my face as I tried to hide behind them. All I wanted to do was to blot out this horrific news. I could feel the hotness of my flushed grimace. The tears—a downpour spilled onto my cheeks. My legs in a violent tremble. My whole body was fierce with the shakes. I had become Dr. Kellman's number one priority for the day. His guilt had gotten the better of him for discounting my complaints. After all, he had misdiagnosed me for nearly two decades, even went as far as having an MRI on my neck—at my request.

The doctor and physician's assistant took the news hard. They allowed me time to digest the dreadful report. Alone. Crying my heart out. My husband came over to embrace me while calling his secretary to alert the insurance company.

"We'll get through this. Together we will," he softly replied.

Hours later, they wheeled me through an underground pass across the street to the hospital. It was all a fog. I felt exhausted from hours of sobbing—spent from this nightmare. A Pink Lady was kind enough to spot me in major distress as Morris was busy checking me into the hospital. She wheeled me to a quiet corner of St. Joseph's hospital. It was there in the solitude, away from the noise in the main lobby, I gained some composure and called my sister Stacey in South Florida.

"ZSt...azczey?" As she heard a pathetic semblance of a voice on the other end of the line.

"What's wrong, Renée? What's wrong?"

"I ha...have a br... brain tumor," I broke down without control.

"What?!?" My sister took a couple of deep breaths

and proceeded to reassure me that I could make it through this. Stacey knew someone—a cousin—whose brother survived major surgery from a brain tumor. She said all this to console, but these strange people and their circumstances meant nothing. Not one thing anyone said could touch me with comfort. She talked and talked while I blubbered on like a baby—no control over my jolting stomach muscles. I told her someone would let her know what room I had been taken to.

"We'll catch a flight and be there tomorrow," Stacey told me.

Not able to break the traumatic news to our mother, (dad was already gone), I told my sister to handle that. Mom took it hard, trying her best to maintain composure. Trapped in a state of shock, she was left speechless.

"Betty, it's Renée," I choked. All at once, I came undone.

"What's wrong?"

With mounting fear in my voice, I told her, "I have a br...ain...t...umor and it's...b...h...ig".

"O-h, no... oh!, I'll be right there. Where are you?"

"St. Joe's," I whimpered.

I met Betty at a party while we were both in our early twenties. I caught her staring at me before our introduction. Betty, in her cowgirl attire with authentic cowboy boots, and me in a light pair of French silk slacks with a matching thin sweater. We quickly formed a bond that would last a lifetime. And forever.

Betty raced to the hospital room. I remember sitting up in bed with long thick hair—a head of hair, unaware, would soon be gone. Betty and I couldn't resist laughing. We were always cracking up at nothing, which explains our deep love and friendship. We thought what the other said was so hilarious. I was unaware of what the injection was in my arm—coursing through my veins at high speeds. It was Decadron 8 mg. The most potent dose of the medicine was needed to alleviate edema from the brain. The swelling could cause a lack of oxygen and kill normal brain cells. It's meant to safeguard the brain from increased squeezing of the tumor, known as intracranial pressure, which provides normal blood flow. Also, I was not cognizant that the steroid shot caused a blast of the medicine, giving me a feeling of euphoria—making me think this was all way too much fun. But there was nothing funny about a brain tumor.

After having me on anti-convulsant medicines for so many years, my neurologist, Dr. Kellman, was most likely devastated. *Where did he go wrong? How could he have missed it?* Never noticing his face, his heavy demeanor revealed such in my first encounter of the bad news with him.

The senior neurosurgeon walked into my hospital room. He flipped a chair around and sat with his arms braced on the back of the seat. Betty and I liked his earthiness. He was, in a way, very appealing. We were both drawn to his serious, calm demeanor—and looks. Me and Betty had the same taste in men. (We dated the same two men at different times before we ever met.)

Dr. Payne explained what would happen from here on out. He talked nonstop, but I was unable to digest much. I did hear the first surgery Dr. Payne would perform would be a needle biopsy to determine what type of cells had formed the grapefruit size tumor and the progression—the stage. Four elongated needles would draw out tissue samples from the tumor. Afraid to know the truth about the size of the lesion, my mind was only on the immense fear— which I held close. Not being equipped to deal with this, I allowed the enemy of whom I never gave any credence to steal my hope. When he steals your hope, he destroys your reason to live. He caused a sense of dread and ran with it. When he wants to annihilate you, he comes in with roaring thunder. No more existence for me. My very presence wiped out.

~

Would You Believe
is powerful and true

~

Chapter 5: Would You Believe?

First Surgery ~ 2002

My close friends, as well as family ties with whom I'd grown through the years and shared tight bonds, wanted to show support. They organized a gathering in my home the evening before the first surgery. Women only. We told airheaded stories of when we were young—lighthearted moments that made everyone roar with uncontrollable laughter—the kind that makes you lose your breath. It was contagious. An intimate group of a dozen ladies. Lots of giggles came with a diversion from what was shortly to come. It was with heartfelt emotion to see them rallying around me. I would not have ended the cheerfulness if it were up to me. But when they all got up simultaneously, my heart turned heavy.

That night turned out to be just the opposite of earlier that day. My whole body shook with fury—like I was caught in a blizzard with barely any clothes to keep me warm—teeth chattering like Mexican jumpin' beans. My sister walked into my bedroom as I attempted to lay down and found me rattling. To dwell on what was about to occur shook me to the core. My imagination—wild. The devil had me. Climbing into bed, it took longer than usual to feel the warmth of the heavy covers.

The next morning was the early hospital arrival time of 5:00 a.m. Up at 4:00 a.m.—no problem. I needed sleep but couldn't tell as I was on the most powerful steroid out there. The brain goes into overdrive, racing at high speeds until the wee hours of the morning. Knowing I could only get forty-five minutes to an hour and a half of sleep, I awoke to the alarm and was surprised at how fast I jumped out of my toasty retreat. No caffeine. Steroids were my kick. Last bath. Dressed—out the door.

The hours seemed slow at the hospital, building up to the OR time of 9:00 a.m. Being ushered here and there with what seemed unending wait times, I saw multiple nurses, tons of technicians, staff members, etc. I felt like I was being shuffled around like cattle. My situation required a team. But when someone shaved off my hair—I came crashing down. *What more could they put me through? I remember the moment so vividly when sitting in the hospital bed after hearing the first diagnosis—my hair. It's what makes me feminine.*

That was the defining moment, looking like a bald man. Another nurse's assistant was assigned to place ten sticky markers from the forehead to the back of my scalp. She colored the dome of my head, following marker to marker with purple. Frankenstein's monster would have been spooked.

The time drew near to 8:30 a.m. I was made ready for the last MRI. I began to quiver like an injured bird—having a major meltdown. As I was standing in the doorway to the MRI room, a technician stood with her back against me. When she turned around, she witnessed the violent shaking of a woman who was drowning in fear. Not aware this was happening; she saw what I was not capable of seeing—I was overtaken by the adversary of my soul. The prince of darkness had me. (Satan knew what was about to happen. I was going to surrender to the Lord.) What felt like being gripped in a vice, I couldn't navigate my way out. Tremoring, like a volcano building to its final eruption, with no way to stop my own earthquake that seemed to come from the depths of my inner being.

"Honey, you need to pray!"

"I d...don't k...now how. I'm J...J...ewish."

"I'm going to say a prayer that has helped me get through so many troubled times."

The breakdown had control over me. I could not recall. So, she wrote this prayer:

A PRAYER OF COMFORT AND PROTECTION

The Light of God surrounds me. The Love of God enfolds me. The Power of God protects me. The Presence of God watches over me. Wherever I am, God is, and all is well.

The technician told me to continue saying this prayer. After getting through yet another MRI, I was wheeled to the operating room. Meanwhile, I kept repeating this prayer with all my heart, until they shifted me over onto the cold hard steel table. The first surgery, the needle biopsy—detected the type of cells. As I later researched my surgery by reading the operating notes, I learned my head was connected to a Stealth device. This headpiece enabled the Neurosurgeon to map out the tumor with gear that was connected to my skull. *Oh, so that was why they put those purple markers on me.*

As I woke up in the recovery room, I heard the voice of whom I knew to be Messiah Yeshua. It was Him! The Holy Spirit was **audibly** speaking to me from the center of the large lesion on the "left" side of my brain—still not yet removed. A window from heaven opened just for me, and I heard with pure calm:

"You are going to be just fine!"

The sound was so sweet and gentle, with a heavenly tone—yet it was commanding. A resounding voice through the hearing of my ears was nothing less than miraculous. *What if I wasn't listening? Hadn't heard Him?* I called out, and He answered. He now has become my eternal covenant promise.

"My sheep hear my voice. I know them and they follow me." *John 10:27*

Although this little prayer the technician handed me was not biblical, it allowed me to usher Him right into the depths of my soul. At that moment my heart was circumcised. *"It is a matter of desperation of the heart."* Crying tears of elation, I kept repeating what I heard from the enormous tumor on the left side of my brain—I'm going to be just fine! I'm going to be just fine!

The hot tears could not be contained—continuously spilling down my beet red cheeks.

"Yes, honey, you are going to be fine," stated one of several nurses at the foot of my bed.

"But you must whisper. Otherwise, you'll get a number ten headache, and we'll have to put you on morphine."

"No, you don't understand. I'm going to be just fine."

I spent the next four days whispering a few words back to only two people allowed in my dark room—on a morphine drip—head still pounding. Yet through the darkness of my sinister hypnotic state, The Lord held me.

~

Would You Believe
demonstrates how Messiah sacrificed
Himself for all mankind

~

Chapter 6: Would You Believe?

Oddities April ~ 2006

God had me on a journey of burning hot coals—my feet just getting warm.

I thought I had been healed, yet something ominous was happening while I was tuning out the warning. Eighteen months post-surgery, I began my daily walks through the neighborhood. At first, thinking it was my imagination, I noticed strange sensations. (My defiance later surprised me.) I was purposely ignoring symptoms, not wanting to go there again. The second week—the odd phenomena began to affect my head. Like I was swimming with no direction. By the third week, it traveled down my arms. And by the fourth week inclusive of my legs. I was almost halfway around the long block. Middle of the day. No cars. Thinking I may lose it and fall to the ground, I decided which way would be faster to get home and quickly turned around.

After seeing a neuro-oncologist, I was told I would need a third surgery. The tumor had grown and become a dangerous stage—a four. I refused. *I had been healed...right?* Previously, the Atlanta team of neurosurgeons told me if I experienced "consistent headaches," I was to contact them. I failed to contact the Peachtree Neurosurgery team. These were not headaches—but dizzy and weak foreboding signals— quickly escalating. Finally, I agreed.

My next and final destination—MD Anderson Cancer Center. A city of hospitals in the center of Houston, Texas. Breast, brain, leukemia, lymphoma, blood, bone, lung, colon, etc. etc. People come to MDA from all over the world. MDA is still rated #1 out of all cancer treatment centers across the globe for nearly forty years. It's not uncommon to see multiple white coats roaming the halls and patients undergoing chemotherapy treatments wearing scarves to cover their lost locks. Cancer is not for the faint-hearted. It affects all people—without choice. Black or white, male or female. Child or adult. Makes no difference to the disgusting cells. Makes no difference your age or ethnicity.

I had a malignant monster growing on my brain—building its nest, one twig at a time. I wanted it to come out—entirely. That was the only reason I went out to Houston. MD Anderson had the capability to remove the tumor bed as well as the tumor itself.

It took literally months to prepare the way there. Fortunately, MDA was accepting only brain cancer patients without an on-site interview. Otherwise, I'd have to fly out there. Breast, lung, lymphoma, leukemia, etc., required the extra trip to Houston without guarantee of acceptance.

Making endless repeated calls to doctors' offices, gathering films, reports and surgical notes all took numerous weeks and months. Not to mention calls to family and friends to keep them abreast of my condition, the weeks seemed to fly by. Five months later we booked our flights.

~~~

It was early in the morning—Good Friday—the same day I was diagnosed years back. Up at 5:00 a.m. and had to be at the surgical center at six o'clock a.m. When I asked my husband to get down on his knees with me and pray, he was kind enough to do this, but I could tell his heart was not in it—he did not want to be here praying in the worst way. Just not his thing—it felt awkward. That was the moment I could tell something was different. He knew what he had to do—follow my lead. This was my brain cancer. My issue. Mine and mine alone. He wanted nothing to do with it.

We were the last couple to arrive at the pre-surgical waiting room before we were marched away for surgery. A woman was sitting and bawling.
~~~

Two empty seats left—beside her and her husband. She was the only one crying her heart out from this crowd of sixteen. Immediately I knew this was God working through me. I took her hands in mine and prayed. Ignoring my husband, it struck me—this kind of life was not for Morris.

She and I spent time talking while she continued to sob. She had a painful life ahead—a glioblastoma— one of the deadliest forms of brain cancer located on the back of her head.

There were eight couples. Eight, being operated on. The spouses left behind to wait.

God had called me, and I had answered His call. I was so filled with joy that my name was now written in heaven. There was no fear. Mr. de-evil could not succeed with me. But with my new friend, he made his way into the open crack that led to darkness.

I was in the lead heading to our specific ORs.

Right behind me was Dericia. We parted ways when we were directed into our separate operating rooms.

Halfway through the lengthy operation, someone on the OR team woke me up so that I could talk. They called my husband and placed the receiver up to my ear. The reason I needed to speak is that if my speech is blurred the neurosurgeon would know he has gone too far. I thought I was on my left side, but the brain under duress causes one to think they are on the opposite side. The tumor was on the left side. But I thought I was on the left side.

~~~

The next day, the meal arrived seconds after I woke up. I was eating with my left hand. *I was right-handed.* Every little detail of those moments seemed perfectly normal. My thoughts were not my own—I was lost. And paralyzed.

Moments after waking up, my neurosurgeon walked in and sat next to me. Nothing came from my
~~~

lips but bits and pieces of words. I couldn't control my speech. The brain controls every aspect of the body, including the ability to talk.

Dr. Ganesh Rao, my neurosurgeon, said, "We got it all."

I was in seventh heaven—over the moon with joy!

Trying to react to say something, I realized there was no way to respond.

"I see your having trouble speaking. Your speech will return in a couple of days."

Of course, the neurosurgeon was wrong.

When Morris and I left the NICU room five days later to take short walks, I noticed Dericia's room. Bed empty. We walked to the nearest place to sit, and Dericia and Tom Patty were sitting on the only swinging bench available. Same thing happened before our surgeries.

We sat next to them. Discovering how stunning everything was, I noticed the bench was high and seemed to jut out—overlooking a monumental entrance. There were hundreds of butterflies in iridescent colors, hanging from the high ceilings attached to strings several yards below—at different lengths. They twirled around from the tall entrance doors underneath our floor that allowed the slightest breeze. We enjoyed holding each other's hands while not saying much of anything. My speech was way too hindered, but hers was not. All I could do was nod and smile. Her name threw me. I thought Patty was her first name but later learned it was her last name. Nor could I copy her phone number. Since I was there for a few weeks, the opportunity arose to bump into her time and again. I thought I could finally make a record on my mobile phone which I'd tried many times but was still unable to get the numbers right.

Morris was with me in body—but not in his heart. He couldn't sit with me while I was in NICU. He could not handle my illness or inability to communicate. I remember he was there for no more than a few minutes twice a day. When he showed up, he sat behind me. I thought we recited our vows—for better or worse. *I need help! Where is he? MIA!*

After being released from critical care, I then went to a regular room for the remaining weeks. It took eleven months for me to speak normal again. Although, there was still a bit of hesitation. It all made sense—the tumor was located less than 1 cm away from my speech center.

Having to relearn to communicate, I took speech lessons at MDA with Gail Davie, my speech pathologist. The first picture she showed me was of a horse, which I called a hammer. Three classes per week and was slowly eking out progress. After a month, my recall of pictures was inching back.

It was in that hospital room I had a male nurse who had a tattoo on his right arm that said simply, John 3:16.

The scripture reads, "For God so loved the world, that He gave His only begotten Son, that whosoever believeth in Him should not perish, but have everlasting life." Instantly, I felt safe. I was in good hands at MDA.

That afternoon that same male nurse told me I needed to clean myself.

What?

Not able to focus on what he was talking about, I used facial expressions to show him I didn't think I could stand or walk. He guided me while holding onto my unsteady gate. The first thing was to brush my teeth. He placed the toothbrush in my hand.

I just stood there—not knowing what to do with this brush. Like being comatose. My brainpower was temporarily impaired, unable to send directions from my brain to my hand—a long delay. Each task seemed labor intensive. Next, he wanted me to wash my face. I held the wash rag in front of my cheek's for about ninety seconds—way too long. Then after washing, I could not figure out how to dry my face. Finally, I was to enter the shower where there was a seat. The nurse had to tell me to wash my private parts.

That's brain damage—I know because I had it.

My Neuro-Oncologist, Dr. Mark Gilbert, asked me if I wanted to stay at MD Anderson for further treatment and tests or go home to Atlanta. Morris and I agreed. (Of course, he agreed to go home.) We both missed our pups. I told Dr. Gilbert I'd rather be home.

"Fine. Any questions?"

I had many questions but could only think of one.

"Doc, you said if I were to receive radiation, I would lose my short-term memory. Does this have anything to do with Alzheimer's?"

"Pick up that magazine and study the cover. Now put it down. I'm going to ask you what was on the cover in a few moments."

I answered most of his questions about the magazine cover but couldn't remember the rest. The front cover had many elements. While Dr. Gilbert was talking, the memory of it all came back.

He explained, "Alzheimer's patients have no memory of what was just spoken or seen. Eventually, your recall will kick in and allow you to remember. You see the difference?" I nodded a slight yes, feeling reassured I would be spared this horrifying disease.

My neurooncologist was a Jewish doctor, who is more than brilliant in his field. He will surely go places at the finest cancer institute in all the world. He told me I would need chemotherapy and radiation.

"Shaking my head back and forth, no chemo," I motioned to him.

He tried to convince me to take chemotherapy but I wasn't having it. *I knew I had been healed.*

Changing the subject, I focused on the radiation. Knowing I was firm in my stance, and he could not win this battle.

With my lack of ability to speak smoothly, I asked Dr. Gilbert, "How does radiation work?"

He then began creating a display on paper to show me how targeted radiation works to rid any remaining microscopic cells that could rise-up again.

"You'll need to return next month with regular visits each month for six months to have routine MRIs, then two months apart, and three months apart until you are released from our care. And you're going to need to continue the speech therapy and writing lessons, as well as build back all the lost muscle mass in a heated pool. A friend of mine, Neuro-Oncologist, Dr. Ian Crocker, oversees the radiation therapy department at Emory University. I'll see to it that he is contacted regarding your case."

Having moved to a regular room where I could complete my rest for the duration of my stay in the hospital, I was then sent back to the hotel—the Rotary House.

~~~

We had moved to town less than three years ago. Piedmont Hospital was located a few short blocks away. I walked there to see my new speech pathologist. Emory University was twenty minutes away. I made a list of close friends who would drive me to swimming therapy—and the radiation center at Fisher Institute of Cancer at Emory University.

~~~

Marrying a southern Baptist man and never remembering much about my own religion, my mother-in-law convinced me I was now Christian because I had allowed Jesus into my life. But that did not make sense. Aware of the term 'born a Jew, die a Jew? Being "converted" didn't resonate with me. Unaware, the Lord was having me hold tight to my heritage—I felt I was a completed Jew.

Excited about the new church I could attend after moving to Buckhead, I'd visited a couple of times with a dear friend who wanted me to go just to see if I liked it. Ended up, I fell in love with the choir as well as the pastor. Although the drive was a long one—it was worth every minute and mile. The over-the-top singers were amazing. With each song, I cried. And cried for two years. They fused the songs together like angels. A choir consisting of around two hundred—half were black and the other half white. The black people would add a subtle beat, taking each song to a higher level as they sang in unison.

~~~

I was only at the church in Atlanta for a short time and our new home a year when I learned about the cheating behind my back. Side-swiped, I wasn't
~~~

aware of what he was up to. Like being cut with a knife. My heart sank to my feet. I tried my best to fight for this twenty-eight-year marriage. *Was he doing this because I had been sick?*

My mentor, Eliza McLemore, who was in her mid-eighties when we moved to town, knew Morris would leave me when I had not a clue. She had something I longed for—a Father-daughter relationship with our Father in heaven. The first time I met her, she opened her front doors and we locked eyes—a radiant glow about her. And she thought the same of me. Eliza sent me a note through the mail after our initial time together. The essence of it was she was so thrilled to have met me. She looked so forward to many more encounters in the future. Even called me her bright shining Star. The times I ventured there in future years she always wrote me letters after the visit and ended with, "My Shining Star."

Eliza prayed that God would send her someone who was Jewish. She prayed for thousands, but not one was Jewish. Her ministry was all women who were having marital trouble. The multitudes surrendered their lives to Christ.

Eliza called it. Morris was unhappy. I would be divorced in the near future.

I'll never forget that first time when I walked through her doors, she led me into their library. Feeling a bit nervous, Eliza told me take off my heels and get comfortable in their leather chair and ottoman. *Glad I wore stockings.*

"Open up your bible to Psalm 91. Now read it."

It seemed so long. I proceeded to read the Psalm out loud. I was totally unfamiliar with the bible.

"Now go home and memorize it and come back next week and recite it to me."

Psalm 91 seemed quite long for someone who just had a large brain tumor removed. Afterall, I could only speak normal a few weeks ago. *Seems like she would go easy on me.* But by the time I had returned to her home, it was memorized!

That was the beginning of a beautiful relationship. She was my spiritual mentor for three and a half years—until she went home to be with the Lord.

~~~

Morris and I had been so happy—for twenty-one years. But the last seven were terrible—the seven years of brain cancer. However, I rarely noticed his coldness towards me as my cognitive ability was not all there. One workday while in our home, he mistakenly called me thinking he was calling his paramour. When I answered he thought I was his girlfriend! He then stated, "I have found us our new home. On Peachtree Dunwoody Road."

My heart skipped a beat.

Was he that serious about this girl whom I had just found out about only two weeks ago? To buy a
~~~

home and live with her? We had just moved to town less than three years ago. I guess that was his plan all along.

Figuring this had been twenty-eight years—this marriage was worth the battle. But not for long. I wasn't willing to stay where I'm not his number one. Once I knew he slept with another woman my plan was to leave. Just wanted to assess his love for me. If I can tell he loves her more, it's all over for us.

Morris' issue was alcoholism. It got so much worse when I was diagnosed with brain cancer. He would return home after being with her, and crash. One night he came home late and down he went in my studio upstairs with the door to the outside open. He could not be woken up from this stupor. He was stuck on the door jamb—door wide open. Morris was a big man. I couldn't move him.

That was the time all hell broke loose. After fighting for the marriage for five weeks—and never making any progress, I fled our marital home before dawn while he was sleeping off a night of drinking. It was clear this marriage was irreparable. Taking the remaining Brittany Spaniel and the Cavalier King Charles Spaniel with me, I made a stop at a big box store in South Georgia to purchase my first laptop. My sister and brother-in-law owned a small equestrian estate in Ocala, Florida. Making my way there, I spent a week recording what I knew was my past life. The writing was cathartic for me, and I knew somehow my attorney could make use of it.

~

Would You Believe
reveals Messiah was a Jew

~

PART TWO

Chapter 7: Would You Believe?

King James ~ 2007

I was delivered from darkness overnight, however, it took years to heal my body. Having had not one but three brain surgeries with all those long hours of anesthesia. The surgeries—and the medicine both took a toll on my flesh and muscle tone. My body had swollen. My weight drastically rose—appearing like a balloon. My skin was so thin it was slicing without any friction from the heavy doses of steroids. It's not that easy to wean off Decadron after being on it twice and for so long. I chopped the pills into small pieces and laid out a week's worth in front of me.

If I took just a wee bit less, my head would pound. This took months. Impatient, all I could do was wait. After a year of lying-in bed, I was getting antsy—a sign I was coming back to life.

I began my first bible study—Disciple I. The class taught the Word of the living God. Red-Letter version. Genesis to Revelation. There would be so much to learn—this would be my first-time scrutinizing Messiah's commandments to the world. Anxious to begin reading, I slowly learned to put the Lord's instructions into practice. Never in a million years would I have expected to be this excited about the Word of God at fifty-three years old.

~~~

My faith ended up waning years later. I was tempted to give up. However, I knew He was alive by the Holy Spirit living inside of me. To throw away my faith in God was like being lost in the ocean with no one to toss out a life raft.
~~~

"And let us not grow weary doing well, for in due season we shall reap if we do not faint." *Galatians 6:9*

In days of old existed many Israelite men who had intimacy with God—and heard from Him. Like Moses—who never questioned God. He exemplified obedience. Abraham—who believed God and was counted to him for righteousness. And Paul, the Orthodox Jew who spoke against the law and later the truth revealed to him; he turned the opposite direction, toward Messiah.

"Did you receive the Spirit by the works of the law, or by the hearing of faith?" *Galatians 3:3*

We are edified from reading the Torah, about those great men of God who went before us. Most believers are of the opinion that the Holy Spirit only spoke in the First Covenant. They would be wrong. And the multitudes think it's not possible to be like Jesus. Look what One man did. He showed us how to do it. The Way the Truth and the Life.

<div align="center">~~~</div>

At age four, I attended Temple Israel in Charlotte, N.C.—even took beginner's Hebrew classes. When I was a pre-teen, I tried to read the Bible. With a lack of understanding, I stopped on page seven. Just turning eighteen, I followed a Hindu guru going on retreats to various locations. It was focused on meditation as taught by the person who translated for him—Love Your Inner Self as One. *Who was one anyway?* In looking back, how could I have fallen for that methodology? And for so long?! The time that stands out the most was the ashram in San Francisco. Waking at 4:00 a.m. and having bathroom privileges a few minutes each, we quietly walked to the main sanctuary wrapped in a blanket. We each had our own white wool meditation mat for chanting— "Ohmmm" for an hour. When you're limited to one sound, an hour seems like quite a long time. Yet when you consistently chant one word, you're automatically drawn into a meditative state. Armed with my own little book called the Bhagavad Gita, I was chanting my way through the book. The goal was to chant the whole Gita, which took the better part of the day. I was envious of those who could do this—non-stop. *Why? What did it accomplish?*

As I continued along this path from the Georgia mountains to New York, San Francisco, Atlanta, and when entering college life in Boston and on into my late twenties. When I had received six years of education in Massachusetts, I moved to Los Angeles, still following Baba Muktananda. Then onto the larger ashram in San Francisco, which held thousands of followers. There was also a massive ashram in Southern India. I thought this was the way to go, as there were masses who emulated this guru. The sitar music stirred me. Yet the people on these retreats were crazed. Not one was sane. I couldn't relate—everyone seemed to feign drama when Baba came near with his peacock feathers to touch them. It was a flood of youngsters, seated Indian style, dot—not feather. They were feeding off each other's insanity—like spine-chilling abnormality. It was so disconcerting. In looking back over my life, I was confused. Did not fit in. Baba Muktananda's only sensible statement was to resist worshipping him. However, the crowd of thousands did worship him—like he was their master. Once he touched them on their foreheads, they became deranged idiots. *Would he pick me? Would he brush me with those feathers? Maybe the spirit hadn't touched me yet. What was I lacking that they had? Maybe I was missing something.* I saw some fall to the ground and bow at his feet in a praise position. Having spent nearly twenty years with this (so-called), guru, I realized there was still a void left in my spirit. *This was clearly a power trip.* No joy. Only arrogance. I woke up from this stupor of immaturity. That was it—immaturity. My search continued... after leaving the meditation mass of fanatics that had entangled me for so long, I burned the books I had collected in the fireplace while I threw the leftover idols into the Chattahoochee River behind our home that related to this false idol. Sayonara.

After being joined with my husband for twenty-eight years, we divorced a short time after I was healed of cancer—my speech just coming back to normal. We had a terrific marriage, never wanting to be away from each other. We enjoyed laughing, being with friends—drinking alcohol, indulging in drugs, smoking pot, etc.—but only on weekends. I had to run my advertising agency five days a week, and always be at my best. I loved being creative. My clients flattered me with their words of accomplishment—and they kept hiring me.

We also enjoyed sailing the BVI's. Twice a year we would journey to St Thomas, the airport being in the town of Charlotte Amalia to pick up a ride to Red Hook Bay to board our home on the water for the next two weeks. It was always a thrilling adventure. Chartering a Beneteau, or Jeanneau, or Dufour sailboat. Those were the best memories. Island hopping on forty-two to fifty-four-foot sailing yachts. After my diagnosis those fun times were over.

But God was sending people into my life telling me I needed to get away from the atrocious situation in which I found myself trapped. I had caught him red-handed. He went to the back of the house, leaving his phone charging on the kitchen counter. I started hyperventilating at the messages. Honey, when can I see you? Baby, I miss you. Where can we meet, etc.?

That was it. I was done with this long marriage. I quietly packed the trunk of my car and literally escaped from the marital home, driving south, relocating from Atlanta to South Florida. Ocala was my first destination, where my sister and brother-in-law had a home that no one ever used. After spending five days there, I realized I needed my family—desperately seeking comfort.

~~~

I did not unlove you overnight, but slowly, painfully, and surely. I unloved you in bits and pieces. With no regrets. I grew a new skin that you could never touch. A new heart you could not break. And a new spirit you have yet to know.
~~~

~

Would You Believe
exposes who responds to the
call of the Holy Spirit

~

Chapter 8: Would You Believe?

One New Man ~ 2008

With my new outlook on life, I needed to find a house of worship. Never hearing the term Messianic, I was led by a dear friend to a treasure in the desert—Mishkan David Messianic Congregation. Messianic means study of Messiah. It is there, I felt like I belong—at last. Gabriel Simkin Messianic Rabbi hears from the Holy Spirit and gives the message based on what he hears—downloading the written Word of God through voice recognition software, into his ears. And it is there, I filled the vast hole in my spirit with love, and with light. I had knocked on the door and sought Him with all my heart. This messianic congregation is filled with His presence. I cried at the Holy Spirit's messages—hit with the truth which pierced my heart. Once a year of attending

Mishkan David was completed—going through the wash cycle by observing all the feasts of the Lord—I felt like I wanted more—needed more.

Messiah is light to a dying world. Light came into the world through Yeshua but look what they did to the light! Men love darkness. Not aware I too, was living in darkness; it took the brightness of His Holy Spirit to deliver me from my dark ways.

"To the law and to the testimony! If they do not speak according to this word, it is because there is no light in them." *Isaiah 8:20*

The Blood.

Leviticus 17:11 says, "For the life of the flesh is in the blood: and I have given it to you upon the altar to make an atonement for your souls: for it is the blood that makes an atonement for the soul."

They overcame them by the blood and by the word of their testimony.

We are given a choice by God. Choose—either life and good, or death and evil. Man gets so comfortable in his ways, it's possible he may never see what is happening to his soul. While we walk in the light, those who are caught up in the world chasing all the shiny stuff, are still living in defeat. The defeated chase riches, while the faithful see this world as only temporary—we are just passing through here. You can't take anything with you. The body decays but the eternal and everlasting will never end. Under the blood is the way to heaven. When we hear His voice, we know we are covered by the blood of the Lamb.

Ever hear of afterlife experiences? People unexpectedly die, witness a great white light, and realize it is Christ? They are told to come back to earth to tell what they saw. They *need* to come back to a hopeless and dying world to tell their stories of real heaven—to lift our souls. That is fulfilling our destiny for Adonai.

Mishkan David is one of those special places for those who are wise to truth and have knowledge above all understanding. It's a place for all nations to come together as One New Man in Messiah. (No money required to join) God does not want to separate us causing division. A house cannot stand which practices segregation, Jews, Gentiles, Muslims, Latinos, Jamaicans, etc. All are welcome at Mishkan David. If you were not born a Jew, you become a Jew just by loving Him—one hundred percent. The word Jew means 'Lover of God.' When we are born of the spirit, the Lord compels us to be grafted into the Tree of Life. We grow branches that bear fruits of the spirit—ripe on the vine. We learn to abide on the true Vine, which is a representation of God, the Father in heaven—who reigns supreme.

At Mishkan David, we are a family of brothers and sisters in the Lord eager to hear His voice— while learning to walk in obedience. We become new creatures delivered out of our sins. Many churches teach once Saved, we now have the Lord's salvation; He did it all on the cross for us and now our part is done. But hold on—that's not truly the case.

You're just getting started. Yeshua had to be sacrificed to defeat death. He had to conquer the devil to show us how to walk out this life—that we too could defeat the enemy with all power. The power to tread on scorpions and serpents.

It is not what the rabbi, pastor, or priest says, but what the scriptures say in the written Word of God. Judaism argues how to keep Torah or the law—called Halacha. They debate each other as to how it's done best. They simply do not know to go to Yeshua because they're ignorant of His way. When you receive Him—you know.

Deuteronomy 6:4-5 says, "Love the Lord thy God with all thy heart, and with all thy soul, and with all thy might."

This is the first and great commandment. Jesus or Yeshua ha'Mashiach added in the New Covenant, "and with all thy mind." These are not mere concepts, but the keys to entering the kingdom.

Jesus Christ is a name given by the Gentile nations in the First Covenant. It has no meaning however, if we experience the love for God and His Son, we can be saved by that name. It takes the cry of the desperate heart. On the other hand, Yeshua means salvation!

Nine out of ten Jews have never read the Torah or the laws. Simply put, they are hypocrites. Comfortable, while oblivious in practicing His way? They say they believe in Torah—the Oracles of G-d, but they don't bother to read it. Why? Could depend on which sect of Judaism we come from and have gotten comfortable in—Conservative, Orthodox, Reform, etc. Or is it because of a 'highly esteemed' group of rabbis who lived in ancient times? Stick to the old ways and you will be untroubled. Isn't there more than security? Bottom line—if there is no spirit in a person, he cannot comprehend what it means to have the Ruach dwelling inside. Once we have the Holy Spirit, His voice will live in you. He will instruct and guide you into all truth.

Why would we want to stay with the old ways when there is a better, higher way? Would you believe there is no greater Rabbi than Yeshua ha'Mashiach?

"But before faith came, we were kept under guard by the law, shut up unto faith which should afterwards be revealed." *Galatians 3:23*

~~~

My father who came from a lineage of rabbis, and two siblings are unaware of His great love. However, at age eighty-three, my mother—unbeknownst to me, was observing my every move. I was oblivious to my mother. (She had already lost my dad.) Had no idea what was happening with her as I had just moved to Florida six months earlier and needed time to sort out my life. My sister had watched over her while she was living in a very nice beach condo in Lauderdale-By-The-Sea. Mom almost caught the large building on fire leaving the burners on. My sister and her husband did not know what to do. They asked if she
~~~

could live with me. Fortunately, that was the time I had just left Atlanta due to my upcoming divorce. My mother ended up accepting Yeshua into her heart as her Lord and Savior two years later at eighty-five. Then she broke her hip and died five months later. I have assurance she will be waiting for me.

We cannot navigate this life without a savior. From ancient times to current times, people have interpreted their own meaning of the Word. God desires for His children to become wise disciples, gleaning greater understanding from His profound Word. The Lord wants us to cleave unto Him for our lives—not trying to make our own decisions. We only have one existence. As humans, we are prone to making mistakes—costly errors. Only God knows how and where we will end up. He knows the end from the beginning.

The Rabbi at Mishkan David follows the King James Version of the Bible from Genesis to Revelation, and only speaks the truth as taught by the Holy Spirit.

Yeshua was a Jew, which is surprising to many. We practice all the High Holy feasts of the Lord, never deviating from the King James scriptures—as Yeshua observed.

Jewish religions and their legalistic beliefs go way too far—leaving Yeshua out of the picture. Gentiles leave off Moses or only read the New Testament. A Jew who believes in Jesus? Unheard of. Christians who believe in Moses? It's just not done. Who says to be a Jew accepting Jesus is wrong? Mere man? The fact is, Messiah was *born* a Jew, *lived* a Jew, and was *sacrificed* on the cross as a Jew. If we could comprehend the meaning of what He did for us; sacrificing His life for each one of us—we would never turn back to our old life.

In my home, as I was growing up, I was taught Jesus was a learned Prophet. That's it. Nothing more, nothing less. I was surprised to learn He was Jewish. I thought Jesus was His first name and Christ, His last name. And He was only for the Catholics. It takes seeking, knocking, and answering the call to become His disciple. Everyone has the call—but not everyone can hear or see.

"Understand, you senseless among the people; And you fools—when will you be wise? He who planted the ear, shall he not hear? He who formed the eye, shall he not see?" *Psalm 94:8-9*

~~~

Why are we here? Why do we get sick? Burning questions, we all want to know the answer to. Why would a loving God want to hurt us? He does *not*. There is only one thing to fear in this life—His wrath. When you don't pick up your cross and follow Him, He will eventually allow the enemy to come in like a flood. The story of Noah and the ark clearly demonstrates this fact. It had never rained upon the earth leading up to the days of Noah. Noah heard from God that he was to build an ark that could float upon the waters. He obeyed. It took a long length of time to construct—
~~~

one hundred and twenty years. People were laughing and mocking at the sight—the construction of the massive ark when it had never rained. What is rain? Noah never questioned God. Noah did what God told him to do. Only Noah and his family of eight souls, plus two of each kind of animal and beast were spared. A female and a male of his kind. Once the rain started, the people who were about to drown, cried—open the doors! Let us in! All perished in the floodwaters— every person and his livestock gone.

~~~

This battle is not here on earth but high in the heavens. A fight we cannot see. It requires a *desperate heart* to allow the Lord into your inner being and be led of the spirit. The bible spells out in several places where there is a remnant of people who will have divine protection in the last days. Their houses built on a rock—not on sand. When floods, earthquakes, plagues, tidal waves, and the destruction of man come soon—those who are left should have no fear
~~~

because they know where there will be no end—a transformation from this earthly vessel to being one in heaven, worshipping in spirit and truth with the sovereign Lord God Almighty.

Revelation chapter 12:11 says "And they overcame him by the blood of the Lamb, and by the word of their testimony, and they loved not their lives unto the death." This scripture reveals the truth as to why we need to be worshipping the Lamb of God— Yeshua. There is a group of messianics, (the remnant) who sing the song of Moses—the servant of God, and the Lamb who was sacrificed for us. Should you believe the living Word of the Bible, you can have this everlasting life. Resist the flesh and give of yourself to walking in the spirit. We all die in the physical, but we don't have to die in spirit. Look around— we are made of flesh. Our bodies aging. We need a savior to rescue us from spiritual death.

This is my plea; From now on let no one trouble me, for I bear in my body the marks of Messiah Yeshua.

God is calling us, every one of us. We can answer His call. Say yes to Him today while your opportunity still remains here on earth. Resist Him—and you will surely experience the wrath of God. Life will not go well for you. I was led of the spirit by the hearing of my ears. Until my divorce. Not only did I stop hearing His voice—I lost everything. My "wasband," my home, my beautiful city, my friends, my best friend forever, the places I had grown comfortable in, the places I shopped, the grocery stores—but most of those things are temporary. I'm grateful they're behind me. Some of the worst years of my life, but that's when my soul was perishing. God knew better what I needed. I've learned much through all my troubles. This moment is all that matters.

Winds of doctrine? It is never a good idea to get tossed about by all winds of doctrine. Catholicism, Judaism with its many sects, Methodist, Protestant, Baptist, Lutheran, etc. A lot of these synagogues and churches will send you in the wrong direction. The Lord does not want to divide us. There are thirty-nine books in the first covenant. And twenty-seven books in the second covenant. We could go possibly be sent in dozens of directions to find what we are seeking—ending up chasing our tails.

It was a slow progression, but eventually, I returned home allowing Messiah to write His instructions in my inward parts. And allowed Him teach me things I do not know through the power of the Holy Spirit. El Elyon, Most High created us. He blew the breath of life into our nostrils. God knows how many hairs are on your head. That's intimacy. God may seem far away, yet we can have this life if we develop an intimate relationship with Him. Sonship. Father-son/Father-daughter.

"Where were you when I laid the foundations of the earth? Tell Me, if you have understanding. Who determined its measurements? Surely you know! Or who stretched out the line upon it? To what were its foundations? Or who laid its cornerstone? When the morning stars sang together, and all the sons of God shouted for joy? Or who shut in the sea with doors, When it burst forth and issued from the womb; When I made the clouds its garment, and thick darkness its' swaddling band; When I fixed My limit for it, And set bars and doors; When I said, "This far you may come, but no farther, And here your proud waves must stop!" *Job 38:4-11*

Yeshua ha'Mashiach is life to all who receive Him, offering living waters and unfailing springs. Christ has not given up on us—yet. The Messiah came to defeat death, teaching dead people how to live. He did not come to abolish the law, but to fulfill it. He came to the earth to set the captives free.

God had to sacrifice His Only Son to conquer the enemy. When Jesus took His last breath on the cross, He left the Ruach (Spirit) in His place.

God was with me all along. He guided me through all the turbulence. Revealing Himself, through His voice. I felt ashamed of all my past decisions. I have since learned that shame and regret are some of the reasons to fall into His arms.

When I was forty-nine years old, I found Him. Twenty years later as I write this testament to His goodness and mercy, I know He has catapulted me far beyond where I ever thought I would be today. Draw near to Him and He will give you perfect peace.

The way I gauge what I have gleaned is by what comes naturally from the last decade of attending Mishkan David Messianic Congregation in Sunrise Florida:

To Love the Lord your God with all your heart, all your soul, and with all your might, And Yeshua added in the New Covenant—and with all your mind ~

The hardest to control is the mind. (I too struggle with my mind) Truly, the mind is the battlefield. Thoughts come pouring in from either yourself, or the adversary, but the higher thoughts are from the Holy Spirit.

To Freely give Mercy and Grace ~

Yeshua ha'Mashiach sacrificed Himself on the cross for us, giving us mercy and grace—a free gift we do not deserve. We don't know why the person acts the way they do—but be willing to give them mercy.

To Forgive—even your own enemy ~

Unforgiveness will make you sick, leaving your soul poisoned and destroyed. Unforgiveness in our hearts will cause bitterness. When we repent before God, He forgives us, and most importantly, He forgets.

Fruits of the Spirit ~

All you must do is commit a sin, then you want to hide from God. Never allow guilt to be a part of your thoughts. God is longsuffering and patient. Run to Him—not away from Him. Learn to walk in the spirit so you can hear from God. Let your fruits be shared for all the world—Love, Joy, Peace, Goodness, Faithfulness, Kindness, Gentleness, and Self-Control.

Resist Falling ~

Backsliding will make you prey for the adversary. Fight the good fight of faith!

Would you like to know the love of God? Allow yourself to invite Him into your inner being. Call on His name—Yeshua, and you will be saved.

If it were this simple, why doesn't everyone take a chance? It requires the "cry of a desperate heart" that gets you eternally into the Kingdom of heaven.

"…His blood poured out for all mankind…"

The End.

Authors Note ~

After I was saved, I spent many years in church as I was not aware of Messianic congregations. It is such a blessing to be attending, what I can say is my Mishkan David Messianic Congregation.

As a Jewish woman, not only can I relate to other Jews, but I have experienced both sides of the coin—finding completion in Christ the Messiah.